Sounds Complicated

The excerpts from *Dealing with Blue* and *Burnout,* originally titled *Riding with the Hides of Hell*, the cover design, photography, stories, and art are by Stacia Leigh at www.espialdesign.com.

ISBN-13: 978-1-7321435-1-7

ALSO BY STACIA LEIGH

♥

Dealing with Blue

Burnout

Hanging Around for You

Distance Between:
Blackout Poetry and Art

To

Bee

and

Bug

and

Shoshi,

too.

SOUNDS
Complicated

Blackout Poetry and Art

by
Stacia Leigh

PREPAREDNESS 101

He'd forgotten how to keep his head
from popping off in outer space.
Why was he here again?

"I... I... I! There were a lot of I's going around." She acted like she'd carried the entire relationship. He had an anniversary alert on his phone, for crying out loud. Especially after he'd forgotten the first one. How was he supposed to know it was a quarterly event? But this last time, he'd been fully prepared.

"Hey, I remembered," J.J. scoffed. "I get some credit since it was my idea to—"

"You wouldn't have if I hadn't left hints all over the place. So when Ron asked me to prom, what should I have said?" Gemma's blonde brows shot up her head. "I waited, and you never asked me."

"Yes, I did." J.J. plowed his hands into his hair and left them anchored there to keep his head from popping off. "We were standing in the meadow, and I didn't ask you the way you wanted me to."

"You ignored me for an entire week after we broke up. No calls, no texts, no notes. Instead you jump all over Suzy. Not once did you go out of your way to..." Her voice hitched with brewed emotion. "...to try to make up with me or to see me at all."

"You're the one who ended things. You wanted space, and I gave it to you. The way I see it, you ditched me, so you could date Ron." J.J. dropped his hands and turned to search the other side through the roiling smoke. Why was he here again? This conversation was pointless.

"That's not true." Her sharp tone snapped his head around. "I already explained how he needs someone to

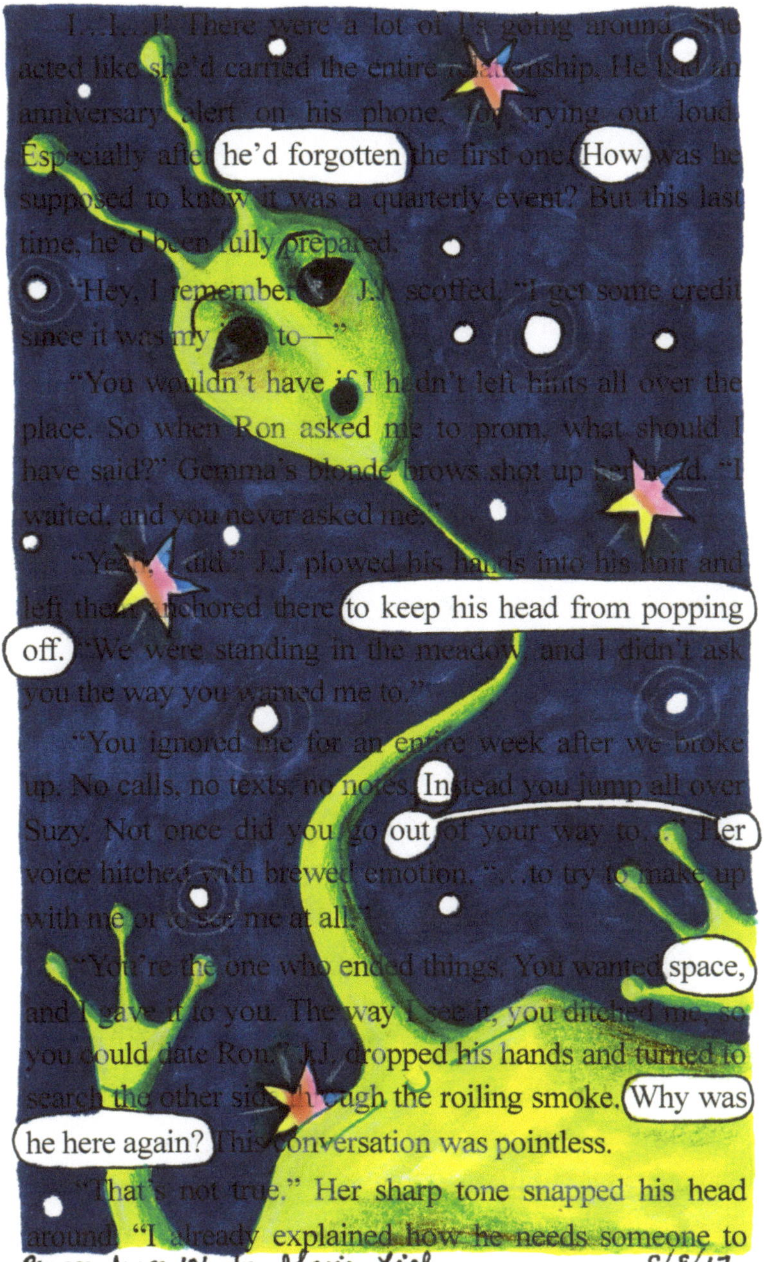

Preparedness 101 by Stacia Leigh 8/8/17

INCOMING LOVE

The arrow tunneled through his back.
Big bad incoming love.

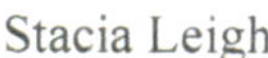

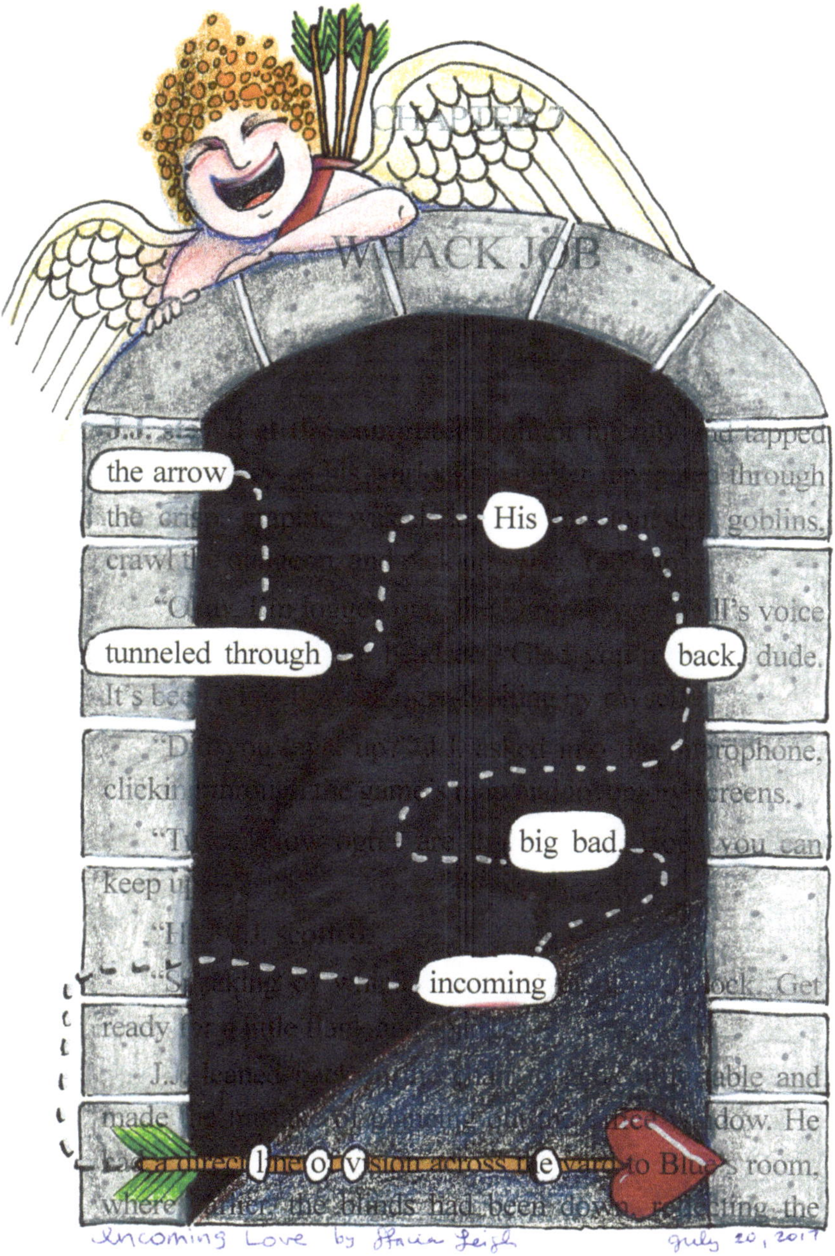

the arrow
His
tunneled through
back
big bad
incoming
l o v e

Incoming Love by Stacia Leigh July 20, 2017

HEART BLOWN

Love blew his heart out.

Suzy banded her arms over her front and braced for something unpleasant. As if pre-prom was the time or the place—

"I want to be honest with you…but not scare you off, you know? I live in a family where we say what needs to be said, and I haven't been doing that, and with you, I want to. The day you called me an *ignoramus*, I almost fell out of my chair…not because it was funnier than hell but because I thought I knew you, and I didn't." He lifted his brows as if he'd asked her a question, but when she only stood there, he shook his head. "What I mean is…I want to know you because you surprise me, and I sort of love you and—there it is. I said it. Honesty, right?"

She blinked at him, fully dazed. He just said the l-word.

"Hey, I'm not expecting anything." He gently squeezed her hand and pleaded. "I don't want things to be weird between us." His words gushed over her, and the long wisp of tense air she'd been holding blew out in a steady stream.

"No, it's just…" She stared. He'd put his heart out there without even knowing if she'd accept it, cherish it, or pound it into sand. Things between them did happen fast, but it wasn't weird; it was right. "I'm not really sure what love feels like, but something good is happening… right here." Suzy copied J.J.'s earlier gesture and touched her fingertips above her heart, setting off a wave of

Heart Blown by Stacia Leigh 8/6/17

BUMBLE BEE BATS

Life will vaporize your daydream.

Dealing with Blue

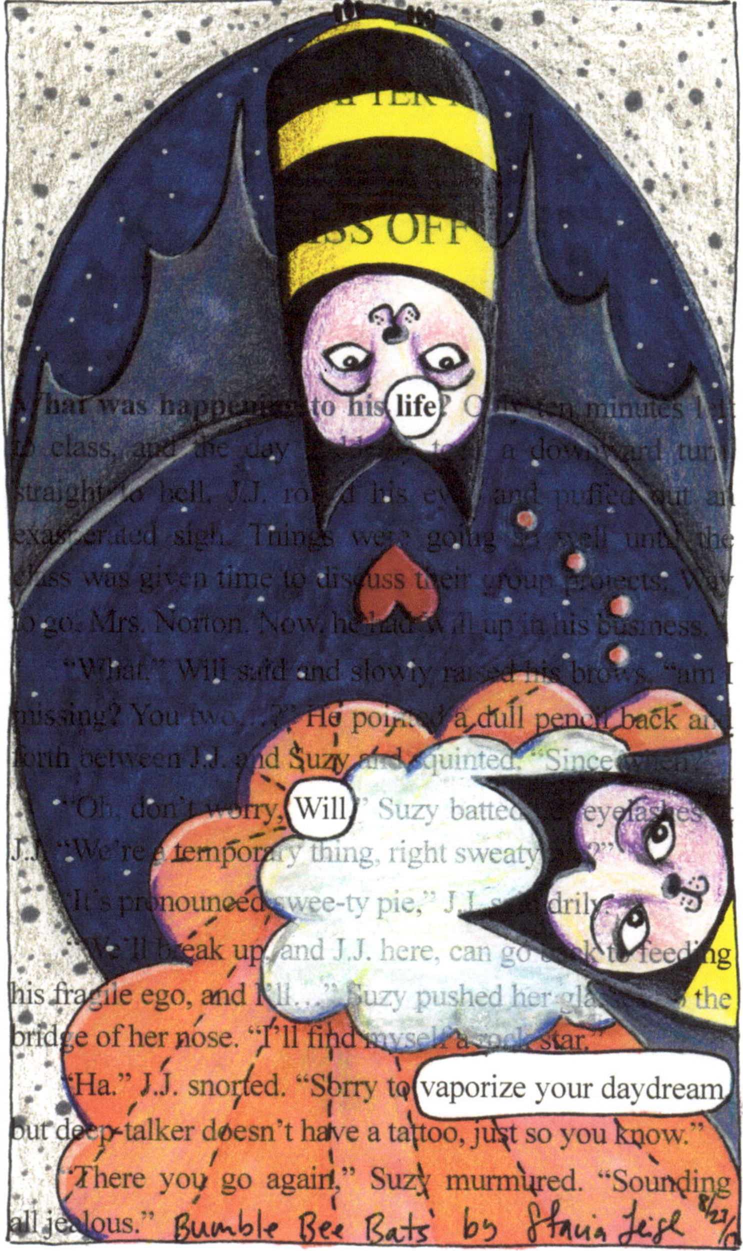

135

SHOULD SHAVE

The Hair Horror Show shrugged and said,
"Guess I should shave."

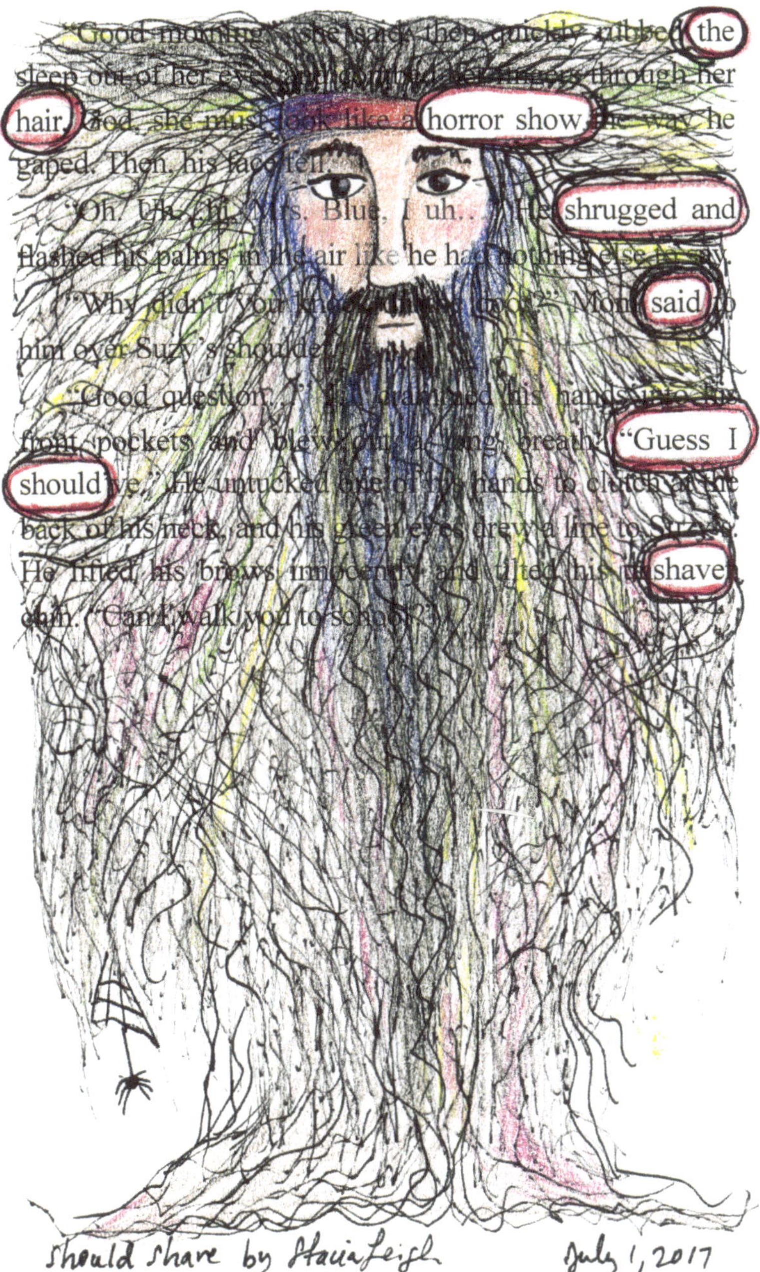
the
hair,
horror show
shrugged and
said
"Guess I
should
shave
Should Shave by Stacia Leigh
July 1, 2017

CONTAMINATED

Careful. Something was in the air.
Something pitter-pattering…
like a heart.

Dealing with Blue

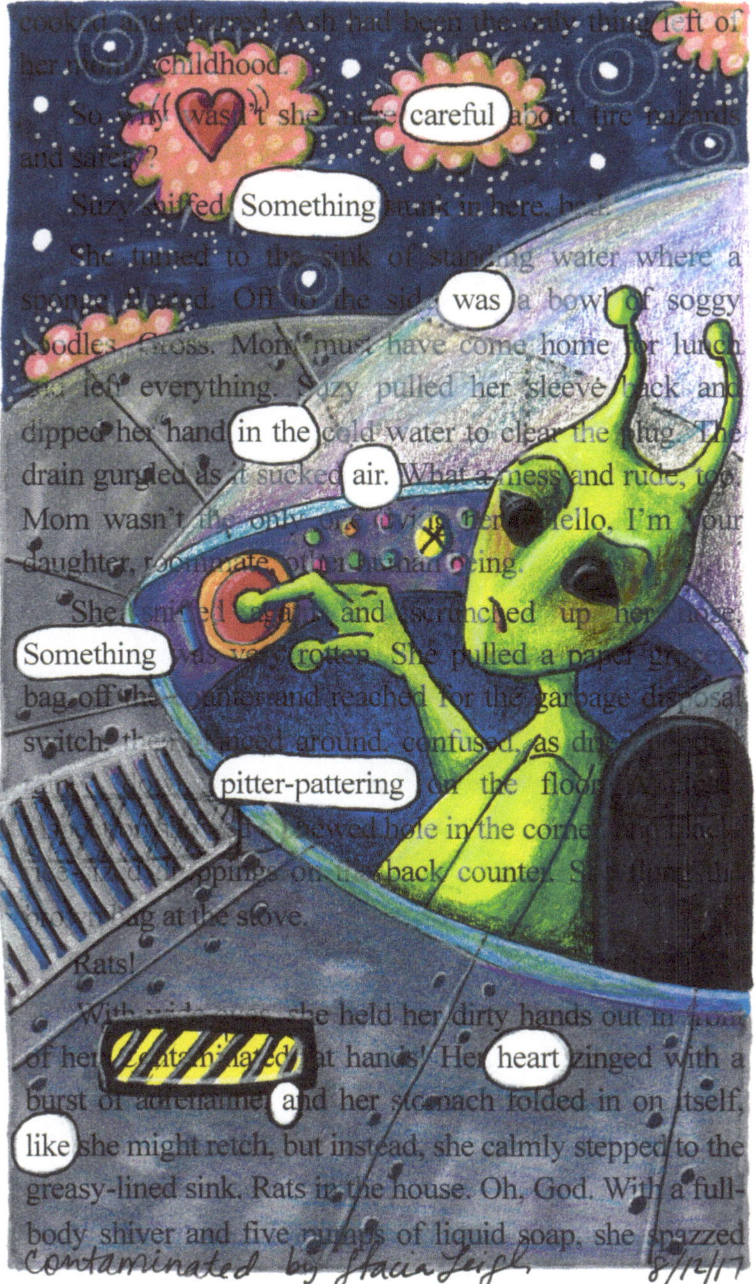

169

SUMMER

That bikini stoked fires
even before summer.

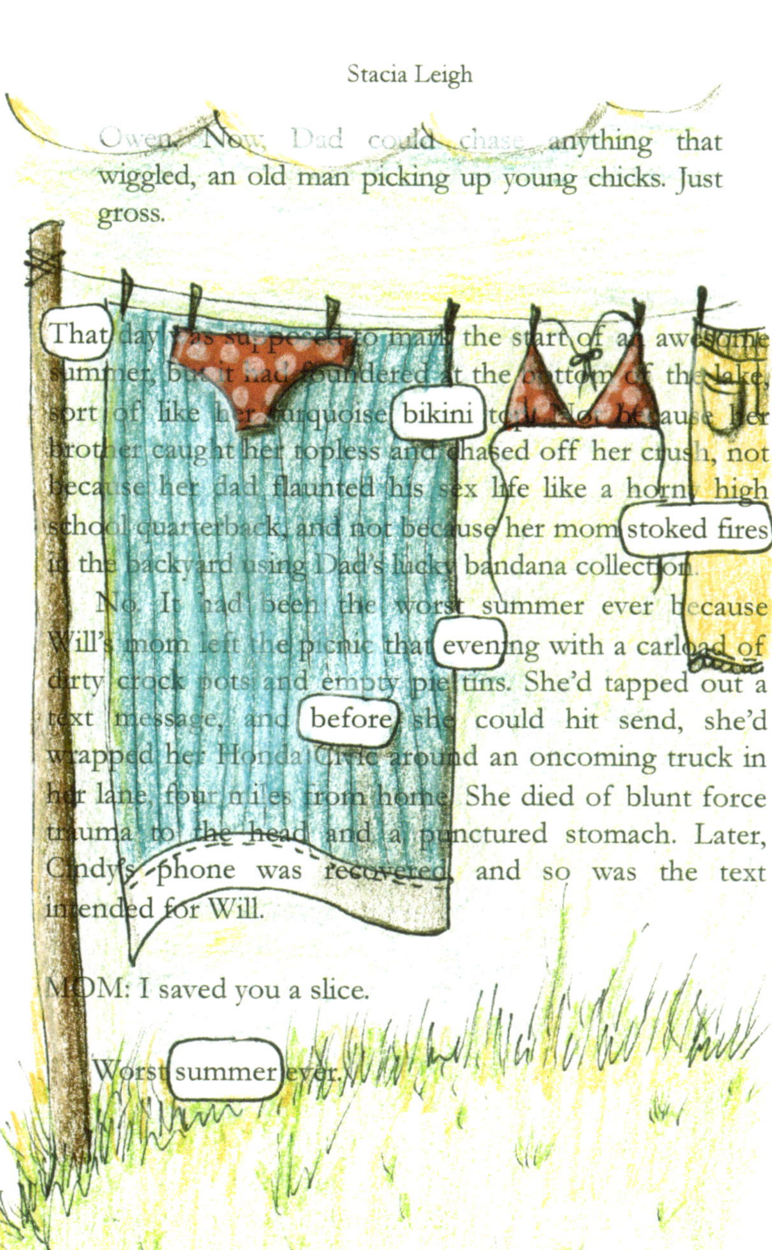

Owen. Now, Dad could chase anything that wiggled, an old man picking up young chicks. Just gross.

That day was supposed to mark the start of an awesome summer, but it had foundered at the bottom of the lake, sort of like her turquoise bikini top. Not because her brother caught her topless and chased off her crush, not because her dad flaunted his sex life like a horny high school quarterback, and not because her mom stoked fires in the backyard using Dad's lucky bandana collection.

No. It had been the worst summer ever because Will's mom left the picnic that evening with a carload of dirty crock pots and empty pie tins. She'd tapped out a text message, and before she could hit send, she'd wrapped her Honda Civic around an oncoming truck in her lane, four miles from home. She died of blunt force trauma to the head and a punctured stomach. Later, Cindy's phone was recovered, and so was the text intended for Will.

MOM: I saved you a slice.

Worst summer ever.

Summer by Stacia Leigh

3/21/2018

RAY OF SUNSHINE

Like a ray of sunshine,
a beaming smile will spill at any moment…

*un*contained.

Normally, the glee on Monty's face when J.J. asked if he could move in would have sent J.J. running back home, but that wasn't an option, not with Suzy sleeping in his bed. Sure, it had a frilly purple quilt on it now, but technically it was still his and he liked that—yes he did.

"Touchy," Monty muttered as the door opened.

Marsha stood there like a ray of sunshine, dressed in butter yellow and a beaming smile.

"Why are you knocking on your own door, J.J.?" Marsha cast her eyes over J.J.'s spiky haircut and black tuxedo. She nodded with approval and stepped aside.

"Uh…why're you answering it?" J.J. asked. He was at his parent's house, right?

Monty slugged him in the arm—"Hi, Marsha."—and drove J.J. inside. "I'm done standing out here. Hi, Mom. I've got your youngest son here, all trussed up in a monkey suit. He's still alive, believe it or not. I haven't killed him yet." He pounded on J.J.'s back with his beefy hand.

Jerkwad. Who was going to kill whom, exactly?

When Suzy stepped into his line of vision, all thoughts of killing left the building. His jaw unhinged, and he stared in awe. Her hair was swept up in the usual way, showing her slender neck, but instead of a contained bun with every strand in place, a mass of curls topped her head, ready to spill at any moment. Her baby blues sparkled like gems against a hint of smoky makeup. He scanned her dress, shiny purple fabric cinched onto her

RAY of Sunshine by Stacia Leigh July 5, 2017

288

HAPPY CUPCAKE

That laugh sounded scrumptious.

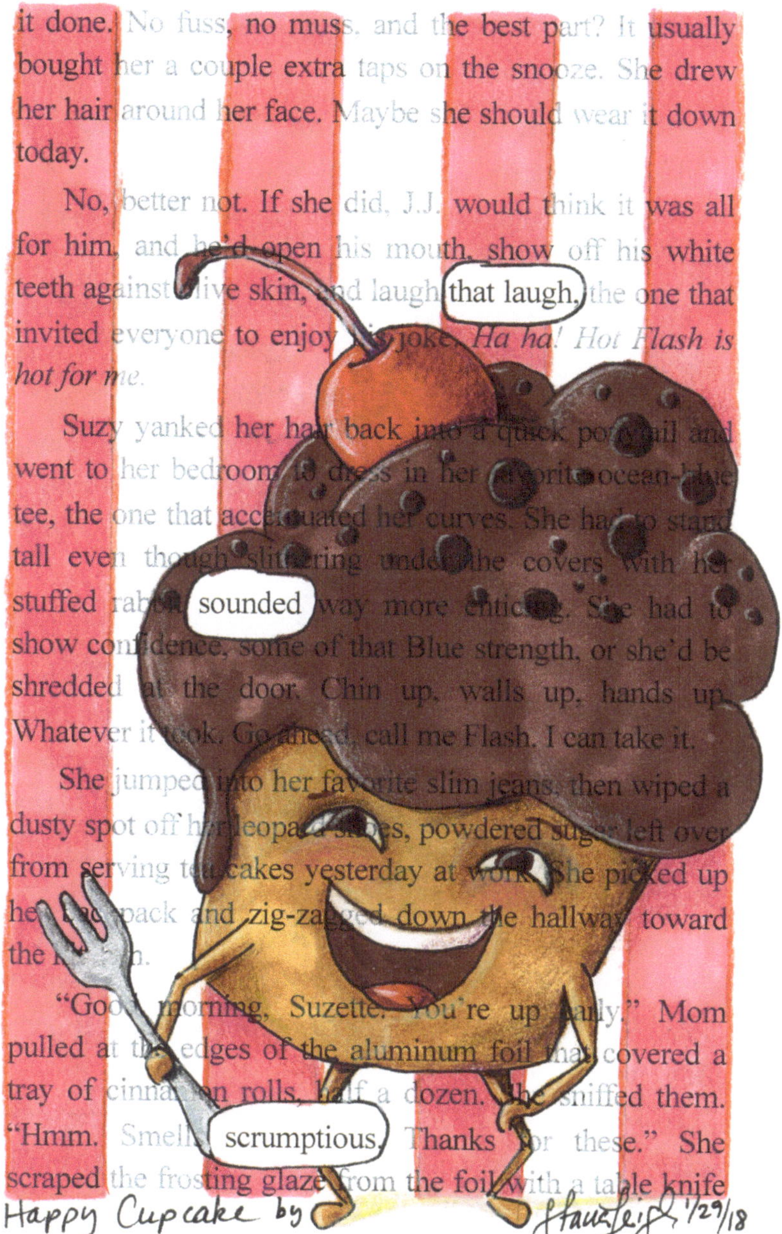

it done. No fuss, no muss, and the best part? It usually bought her a couple extra taps on the snooze. She drew her hair around her face. Maybe she should wear it down today.

No, better not. If she did, J.J. would think it was all for him, and he'd open his mouth, show off his white teeth against olive skin, and laugh that laugh, the one that invited everyone to enjoy his joke. *Ha ha! Hot Flash is hot for me.*

Suzy yanked her hair back into a quick ponytail and went to her bedroom to dress in her favorite ocean-blue tee, the one that accentuated her curves. She had to stand tall even though slithering under the covers with her stuffed rabbit sounded way more enticing. She had to show confidence, some of that Blue strength, or she'd be shredded at the door. Chin up, walls up, hands up. Whatever it took. Go ahead, call me Flash. I can take it.

She jumped into her favorite slim jeans, then wiped a dusty spot off her leopard shoes, powdered sugar left over from serving teacakes yesterday at work. She picked up her backpack and zig-zagged down the hallway toward the kitchen.

"Good morning, Suzette. You're up early." Mom pulled at the edges of the aluminum foil that covered a tray of cinnamon rolls, half a dozen. She sniffed them. "Hmm. Smells scrumptious. Thanks for these." She scraped the frosting glaze from the foil with a table knife

Happy Cupcake by Stacy Leigh 1/29/18

WAKE UP

You're going to wake up with disbelief,
because you see me.

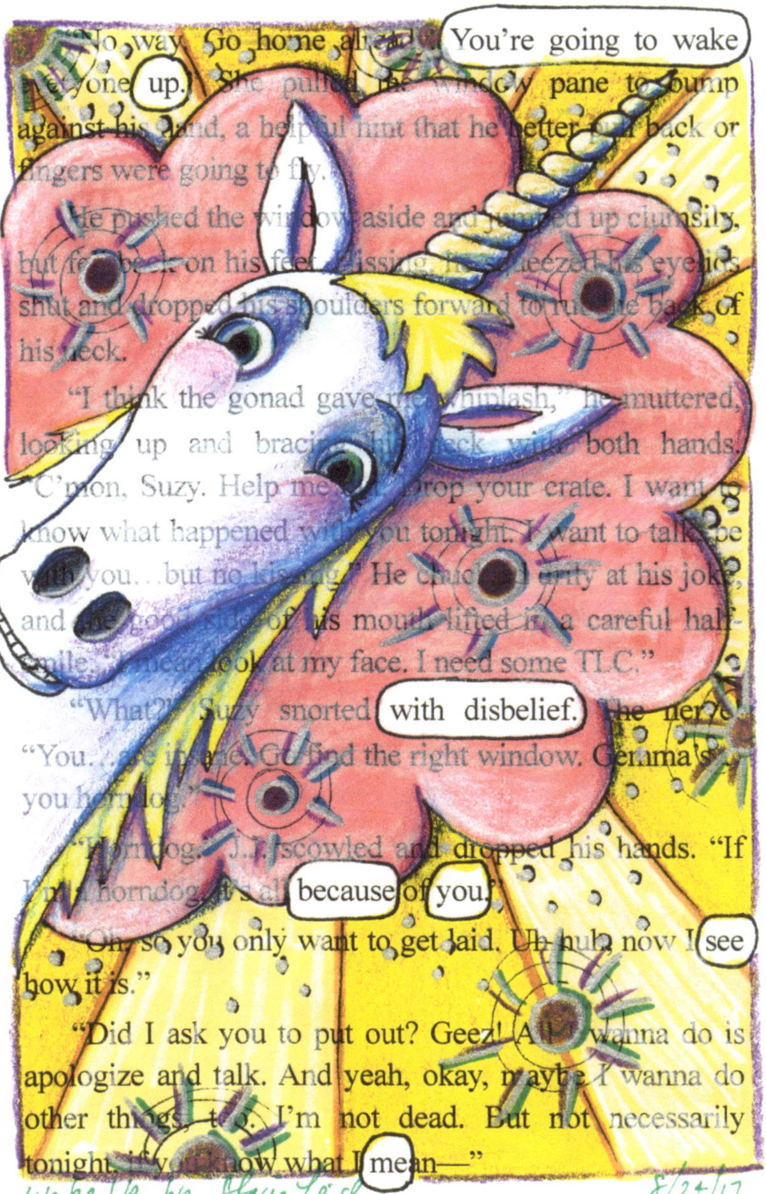

"No way. Go home already. You're going to wake everyone up." She pulled the window pane to bump against his hand, a helpful hint that he better pull back or fingers were going to fly.

He pushed the window aside and jumped up clumsily, but fell back on his feet, hissing. He squeezed his eyelids shut and dropped his shoulders forward to rub the back of his neck.

"I think the gonad gave me whiplash," he muttered, looking up and bracing his neck with both hands. "C'mon, Suzy. Help me. Drop your crate. I want to know what happened with you tonight. I want to talk, be with you…but no kissing." He chuckled dryly at his joke, and the good side of his mouth lifted in a careful half-smile. "I mean, look at my face. I need some TLC."

"What?" Suzy snorted with disbelief. The nerve. "You…are insane. Go find the right window. Gemma's s[illegible] you horndog."

"Horndog." J.J. scowled and dropped his hands. "If I'm a horndog, it's all because of you."

"Oh, so you only want to get laid. Uh-huh, now I see how it is."

"Did I ask you to put out? Geez! All I wanna do is apologize and talk. And yeah, okay, maybe I wanna do other things, too. I'm not dead. But not necessarily tonight, if you know what I mean—"

Wake Up by Stacy Leigh 8/24/17

IT'S COMPLICATED

He ordered a large side of feeling
and the avoidance maneuver roll
since they were sharing a can of love.

Dealing with Blue

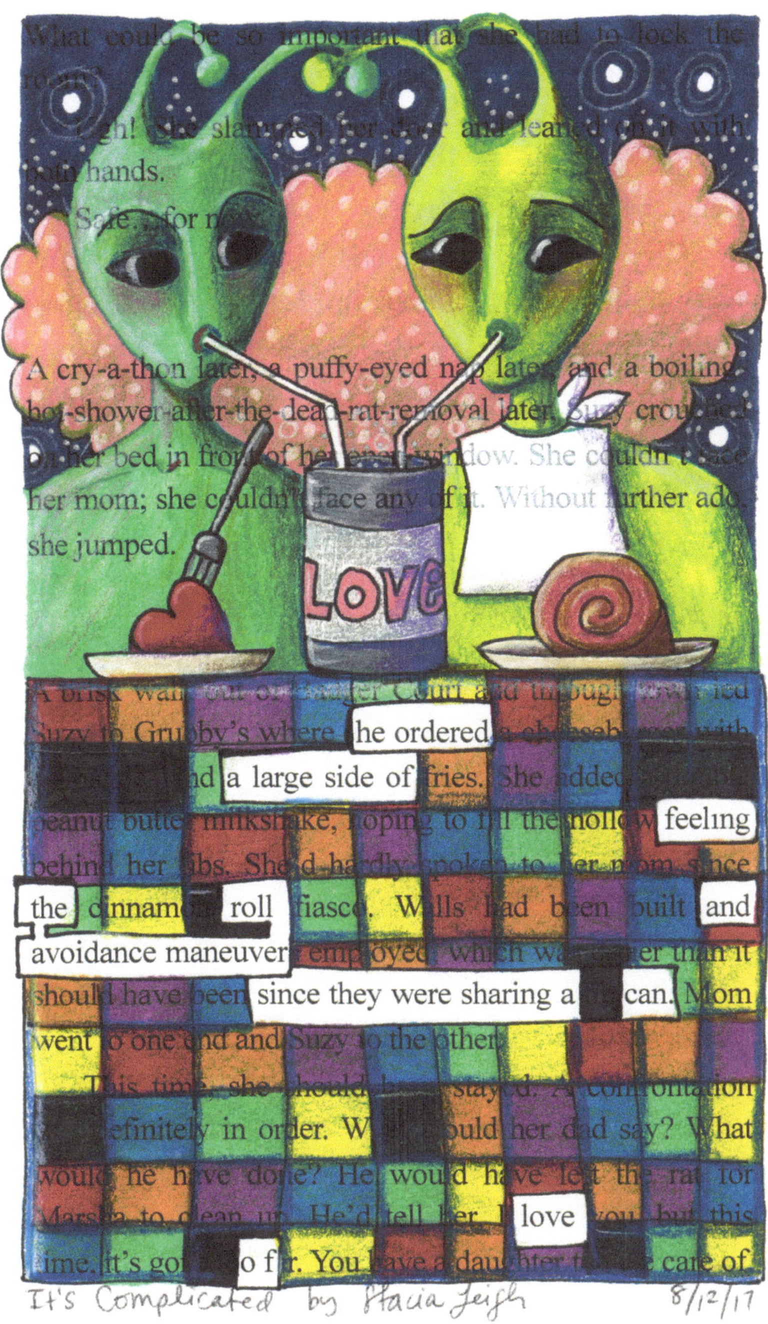

ALTERED

They kissed,
and his music
altered her heart.

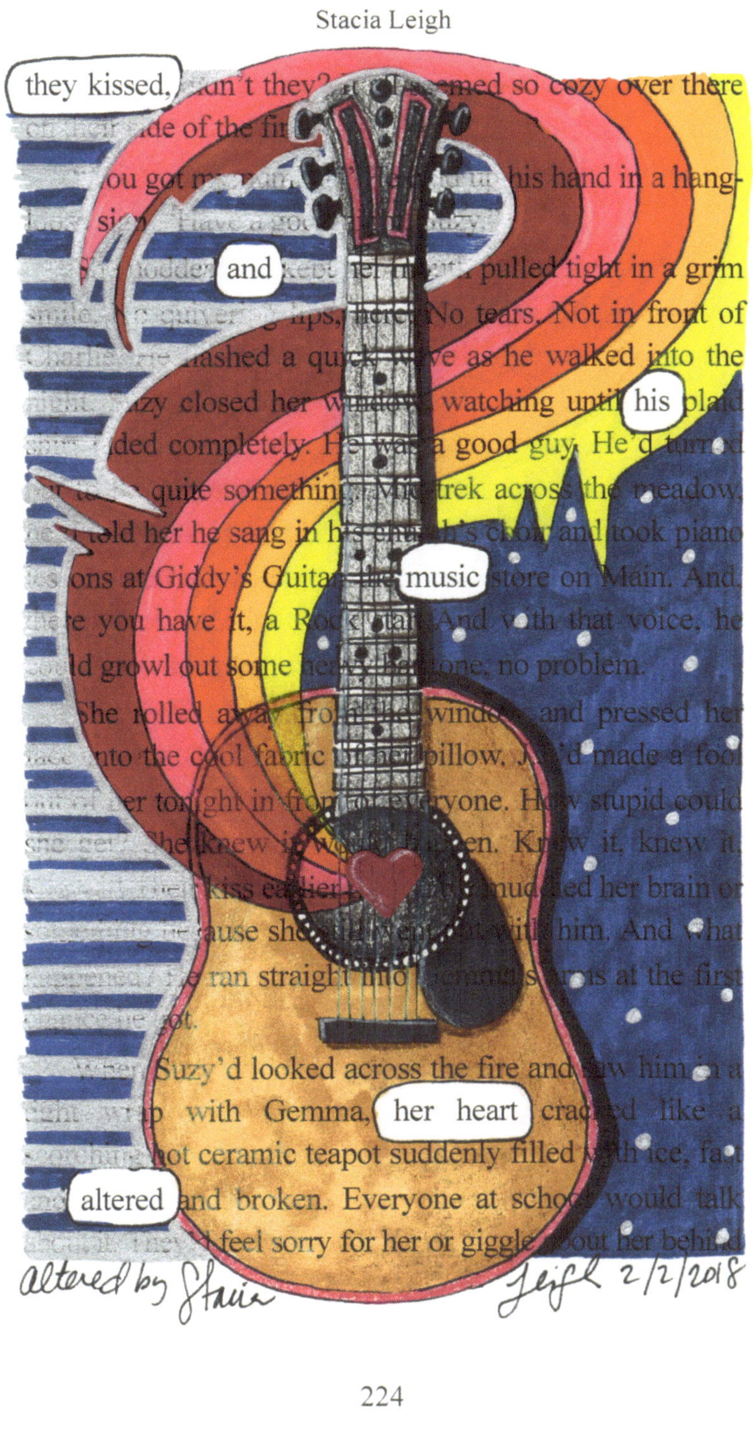

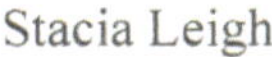

Stacia Leigh

they kissed,

and

his

music

her heart

altered

altered by Stacia Leigh 2/2/2018

224

WAITED FOR THE LIGHT

The big fool waited for the light,
half aware of the kiss.

assuming a hot date with you is eating cold fries at Grubby's."

"Why don't you ever wear your hair down?" He gently tugged the end of her ponytail. "It's long. I didn't realize it until you opened your window and put it all out there this morning."

"I knew it!" They hadn't even left Badger Court, and he was already starting with the jokes. "Just drop it. That was an accident," she bit out, stomping ahead of him as they cut to the paved drive.

If he teased her again, she'd explode. Talk about festering emotions. Ugh! She clenched her fists. The big blow-up with Mom left her hollowed out and thin, like an onion skin. What if she started crying? Then, she'd really make a fool out of herself.

J.J. touched her arm at the corner as they waited for the light to turn green.

"Before I forget, what's your number?" he asked, unfazed by her temper. He nudged her with his elbow and typed in the digits as she curtly rattled them off. The light turned, and she stepped off the curb to cross the street, only half aware of the students, buses, and cars that came from every direction toward the school. J.J. caught up to her and said, "I'll text you later."

"Sure you will." Suzy pulled away from him to merge with the herd into Overdale High, when a warm palm slipped into hers and lured her back. In the middle of the sidewalk J.J. kissed her temple and breathed in.

127

Waited for the Light by Alexia Leigh

4/21/17

THE BOOT

He was busy getting his boot grounded
for new memories.

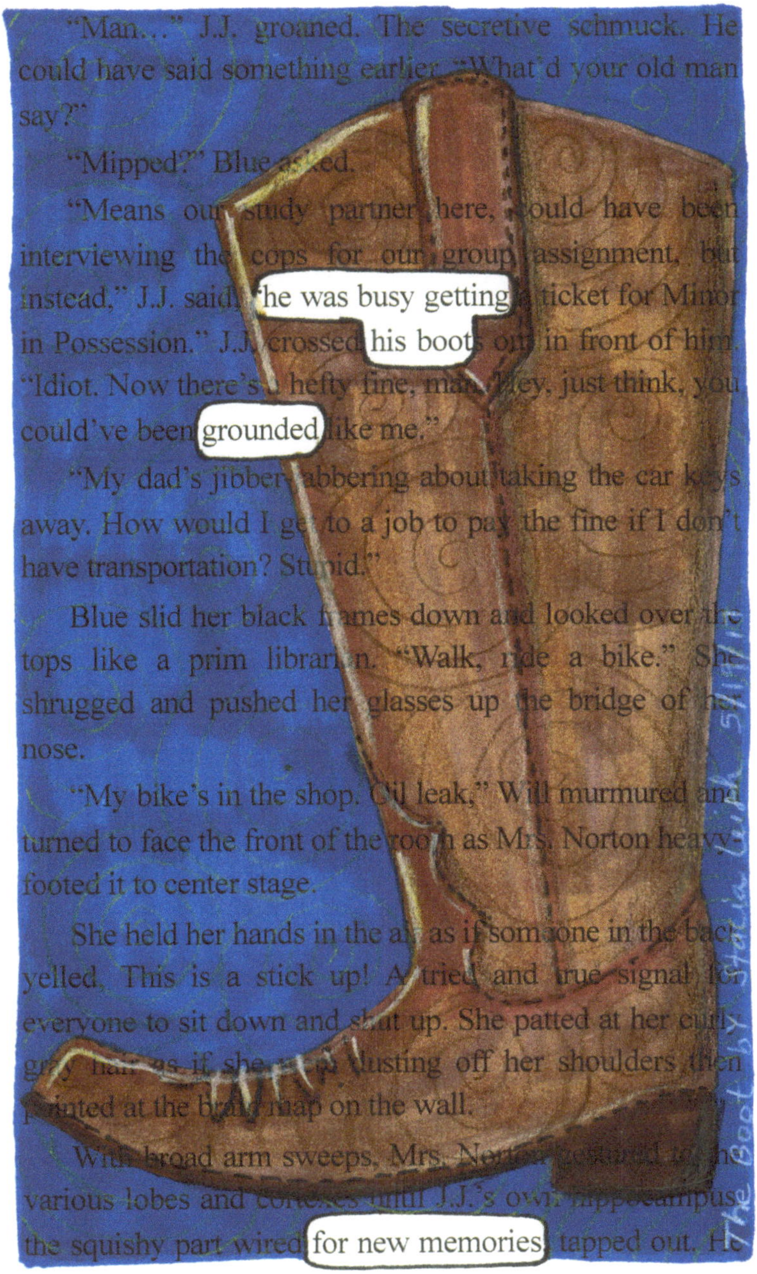

"Man…" J.J. groaned. The secretive schmuck. He could have said something earlier. "What'd your old man say?"

"Mipped?" Blue asked.

"Means our study partner here, could have been interviewing the cops for our group assignment, but instead," J.J. said, "he was busy getting a ticket for Minor in Possession." J.J. crossed his boots out in front of him. "Idiot. Now there's a hefty fine, man. Hey, just think, you could've been grounded like me."

"My dad's jibber-jabbering about taking the car keys away. How would I get to a job to pay the fine if I don't have transportation? Stupid."

Blue slid her black frames down and looked over the tops like a prim librarian. "Walk, ride a bike." She shrugged and pushed her glasses up the bridge of her nose.

"My bike's in the shop. Oil leak," Will murmured and turned to face the front of the room as Mrs. Norton heavy-footed it to center stage.

She held her hands in the air as if someone in the back yelled, This is a stick up! A tried and true signal for everyone to sit down and shut up. She patted at her curly gray hair as if she were dusting off her shoulders then pointed at the brain map on the wall.

With broad arm sweeps, Mrs. Norton gestured to the various lobes and cortexes until J.J.'s own hippocampus, the squishy part wired for new memories, tapped out. He

The Boot by Stacia Leigh 5/19/11

THROUGH THE SEA

Through a sea of disappointment,
she caught someone's eyes on her.

Dealing with Blue

really bad. One smack was all he needed to put Will flat on his gaming cushion. Lights out.

"Dude's jealous. Look at him, Blue." Will laughed like a braying donkey. "His face is as red as your hair."

"J.J., are you feeling a *little* jealous?" Suzy mocked him with a light-hearted grin. "It's normal. I don't mind."

"I don't sound like that." J.J. smirked. Funny girl. He turned to Will. "And for your information, Suzy and I are official—"

"J.J.!" Gemma's voice cut through the air.

"—scorchers." J.J. turned as his ex and The Mouth pushed through a sea of flannel and denim to stand in front of them. Holly crossed her arms and shook her head with disappointment as if she'd caught him stealing brews out of someone else's cooler.

"Hey," he said warily and crammed his hands into his jacket pockets. "What's up?"

"J.J., I need to talk to you...alone." Gemma nodded to the other side of the fire, her eyes pleading with his.

Alone? What for? After driving with Suzy yesterday, he'd gone straight home, and before peeling off his wet clothes, he'd called Gemma. He told her straight up there was no more thinking about it. They were over, and she'd hung up on him. So he'd taken that to mean message received. Stick a fork in it…done.

"Nah, I don't think so," J.J. said. "I'm here with my girl."

through the sea by Stacia Leigh 6.21.17

213

STATIC

His heart turned off
when his mind needed to listen.

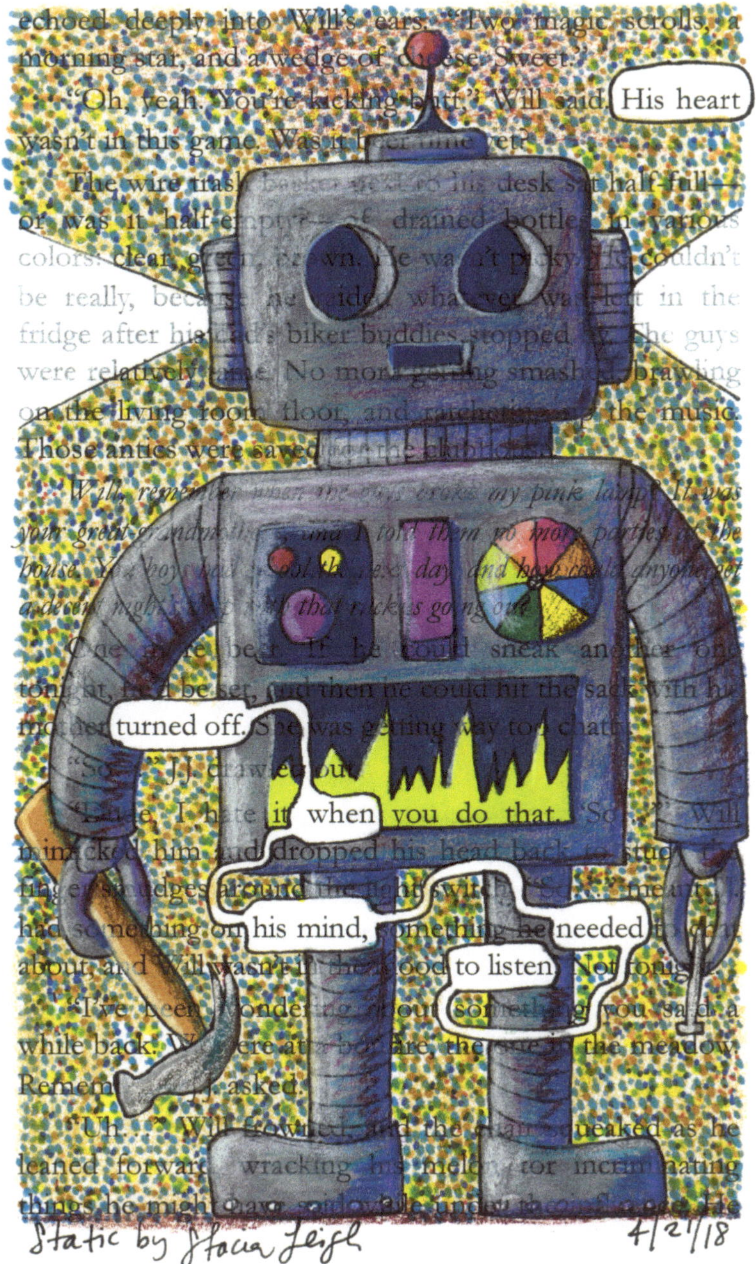
His heart
turned off.
when you do that.
his mind,
needed
to listen.
Static by Stacia Leigh
4/21/18

SAY THE WORD

A horrible idea was regret.
Say the word…tender, pulsing.

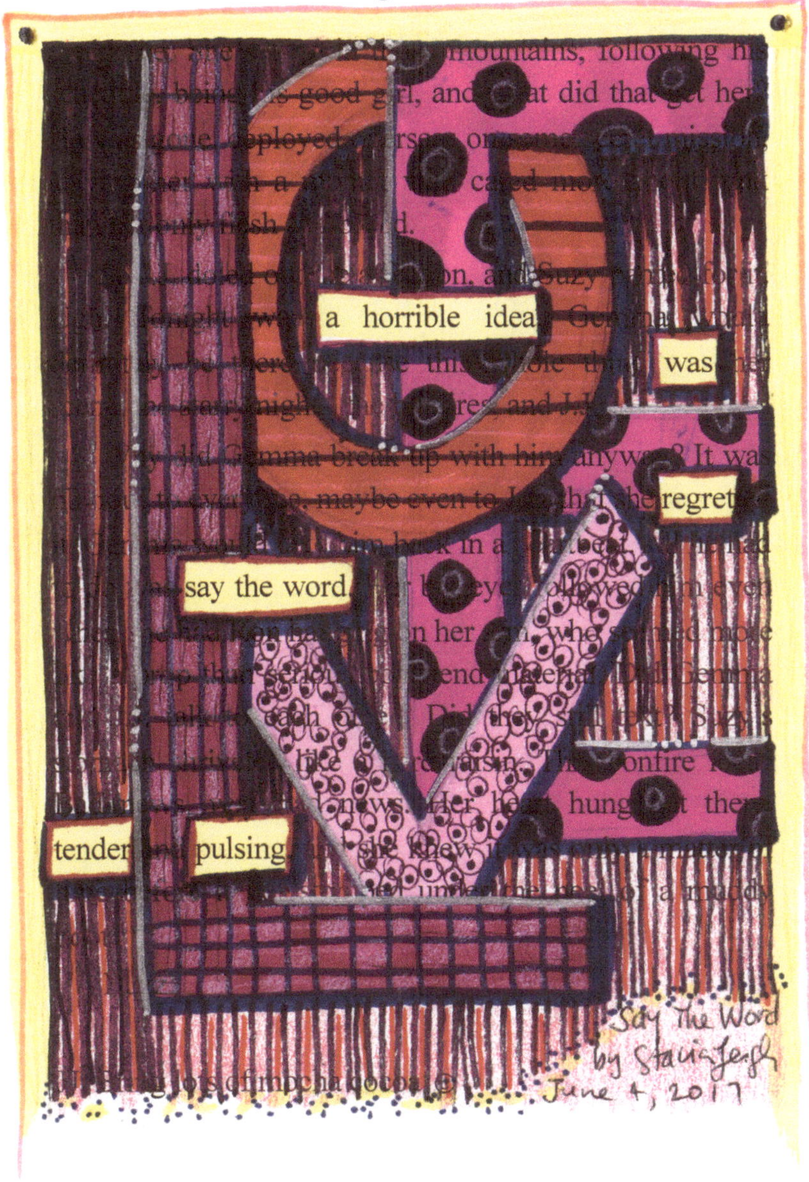
a horrible idea
was
regret
say the word
tender
pulsing
Say The Word
by Stacia Leigh
June 4, 2017

ON THE TABLE

You're my partner, my neighbor.
We're together all the time…
on the table.
But I might need more of you.

Dealing with Blue

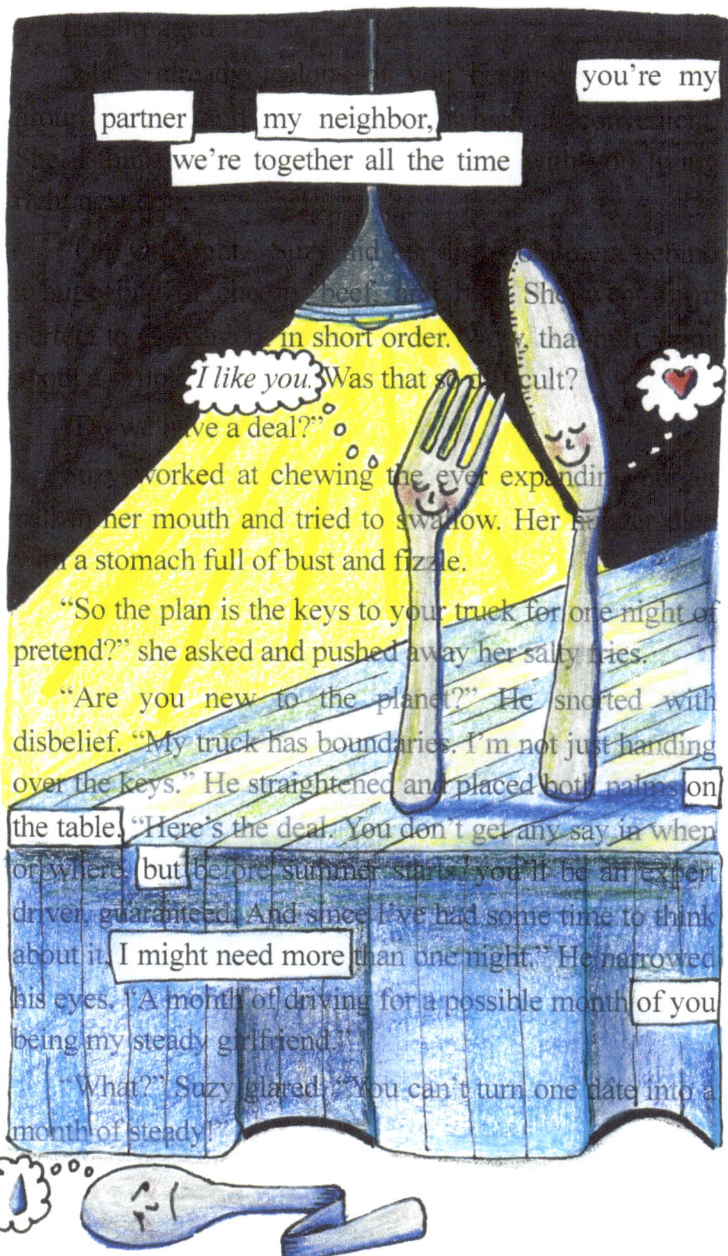

83

On the Table by Stacie Leigh 8/6/2017

DARK CORNER

No Apologies stared into the dark corner of hell,
forever carrying tears,
while Fun kept on walking.

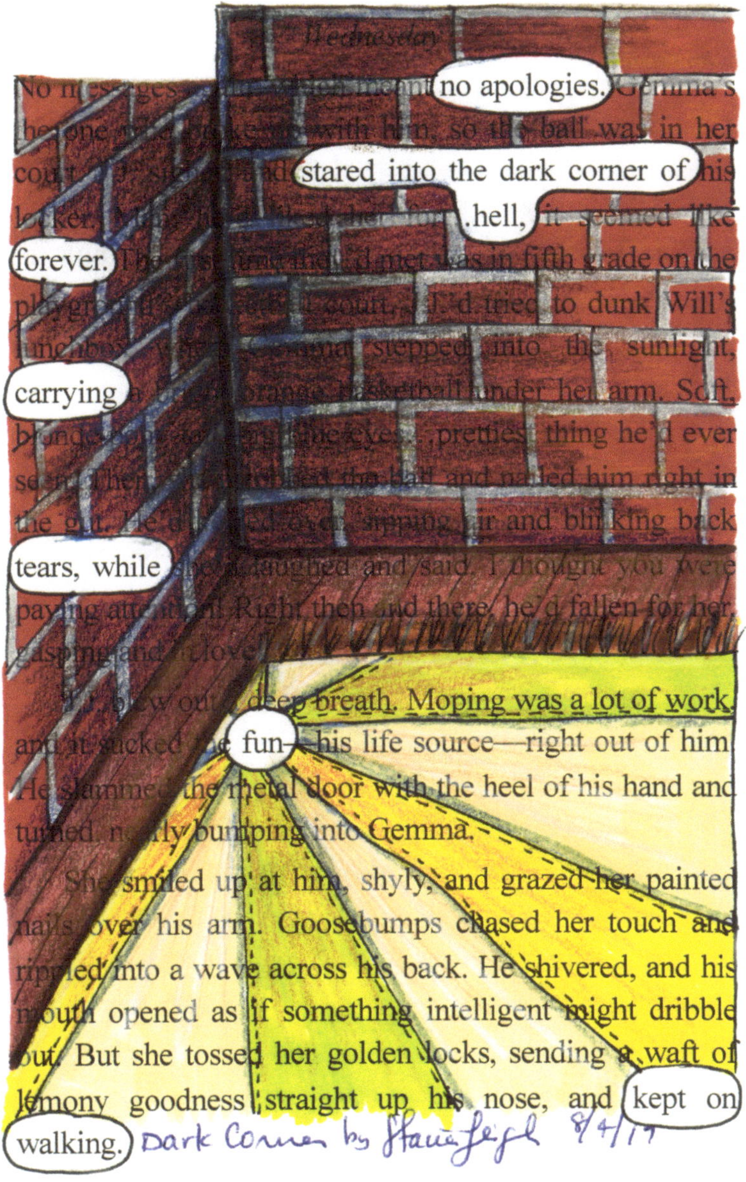
no apologies.
stared into the dark corner of
hell,
forever.
carrying
tears, while
fun
kept on
walking.
Dark Corner by Stacia Leigh 8/4/17

WHAT MY DOG THINKS

You ran away,
proof that your heart could forget me.

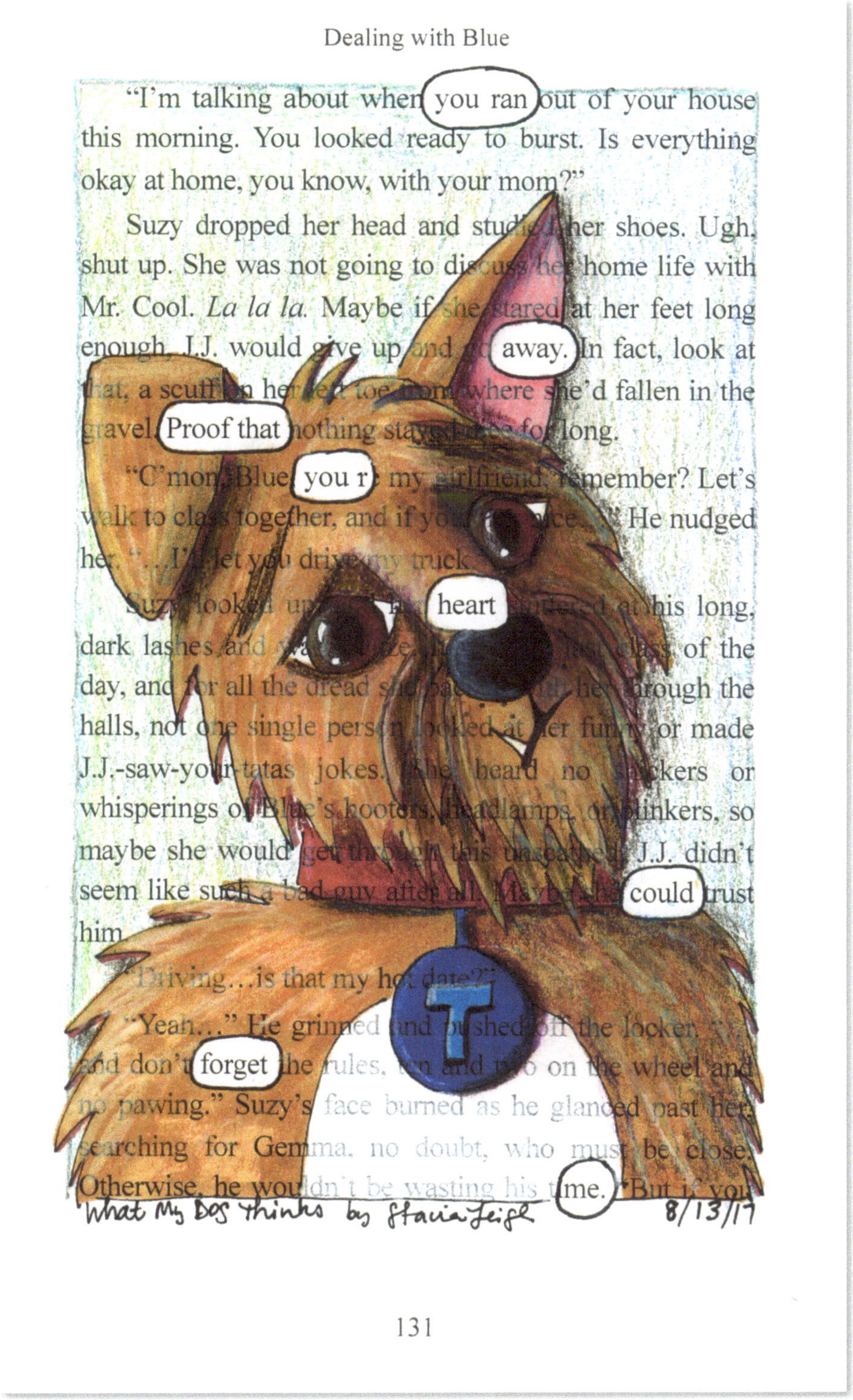

"I'm talking about when you ran out of your house this morning. You looked ready to burst. Is everything okay at home, you know, with your mom?"

Suzy dropped her head and studied her shoes. Ugh, shut up. She was not going to discuss her home life with Mr. Cool. *La la la.* Maybe if she stared at her feet long enough, J.J. would give up and [illegible] away. In fact, look at that, a scuff on her left toe from where she'd fallen in the gravel. Proof that nothing stayed [illegible] for long.

"C'mon, Blue, you r[illegible] my girlfriend, remember? Let's walk to class together, and if you [illegible] nice..." He nudged her. "...I'll let you drive my truck."

Suzy looked up [illegible] heart [illegible] at his long, dark lashes and [illegible] class of the day, and for all the dread she [illegible] through the halls, not one single person looked at her funny or made J.J.-saw-your-tatas jokes. She heard no snickers or whisperings of Blue's hooters, headlamps, or blinkers, so maybe she would get through this unscathed. J.J. didn't seem like such a bad guy after all. Maybe she could trust him.

"Driving...is that my hot date?"

"Yeah..." He grinned and pushed off the locker. "[illegible] and don't forget the rules, ten and two on the wheel and no pawing." Suzy's face burned as he glanced past her, searching for Gemma, no doubt, who must be close. Otherwise, he wouldn't be wasting his time." But if you

What My Dog thinks by Stacia Leigh 8/13/17

MY SPACE

It meant something good
when it was over.
I need my space.

ago, it might have even meant *something.* But now? He shot a look through the shimmering heat tripping up on Suzy's blue gaze, and he jerked his hand free.

"Spill it," he said curtly, twisting back to Gemma. Forget it. He should walk away.

"Don't worry about her. She's got Will, and now, Charlie, too. The girl moves fast."

Charlie! J.J. craned his neck to see Will slapping the good ol' mysterious Up Chuck on the back like they were besties. J.J. curled his lip, ready to snarl, and just as quickly, his face dropped. No, no, no. Suzy threw her head back, laughing at something chuckhole said.

"What do you want with me?" he said impatiently. "You told me to think about it, and I did. When I told you it was over, you hung up on me. So now what?"

"J.J., come on. I don't want to fight." Her palms flew out to him. "I want to make up. Why aren't we back together right now? It's been so long. I miss you."

"Miss me, huh? You've been jerking me around for weeks, *I miss you, I want you, but I need my space. I need you. I love you, but I'm with Ron.*"

"Ron's not the issue. We broke up because I always have to make the first move, like now." She swished her hand through the air, ready to lay down a full catalog of his misdeeds. "I call you. I say I love you. I meet you at your locker. I plan time to be with you. In fact, I have to tell you when it's our anniversary."

My Space by Stacia Leigh 8/9/11

216

THE HONEST TRUTH

Where had things gone so wrong?
The honest truth was something
locked in the past.

shoulder against the metal door, trying to act casual, while a cloudy mist of love and excitement gassed his cranium.

"I miss you," he said. It was the honest truth, too. Where had things gone so wrong? They were on day five, and what used to come naturally, like growling her name to hear her laugh and asking everyday questions like How was basketball practice? or What'd your dad say this time? now seemed awkward and tense. J.J. wanted to say something perfect. Something to put them back to the way they were.

"I miss you, too," Gemma said and tickled her pink nails up his arm. A bubble of warmth engulfed him from top to toe, and the loud voices, the rattling locker doors, the shuffling and slamming, all drifted away.

"Before, you said—" J.J. started.

"I want to—oh sorry. Go ahead." Gemma's cheeks turned a rosy pink, and she laughed, making J.J.'s pulse quicken.

"No, you first." He grinned.

"I want to…" Gemma bit her lip and blinked up at him from under her thick, black lashes. "What about us getting back together? I miss the way we were." She squeezed his hand, her eyes on his. "What do you think?"

"Me, too." He swallowed past the tension blocking his throat, and relief percolated up through his body.

"The only thing is, prom." Gemma opened her palms and gave him a sheepish look. "Ron asked me to prom, and I sorta…I was mad at you, so I said yes. But, it's

The Honest Truth by Stacia Leigh 7/28/17

58

REALITY

Reality wouldn't budge.

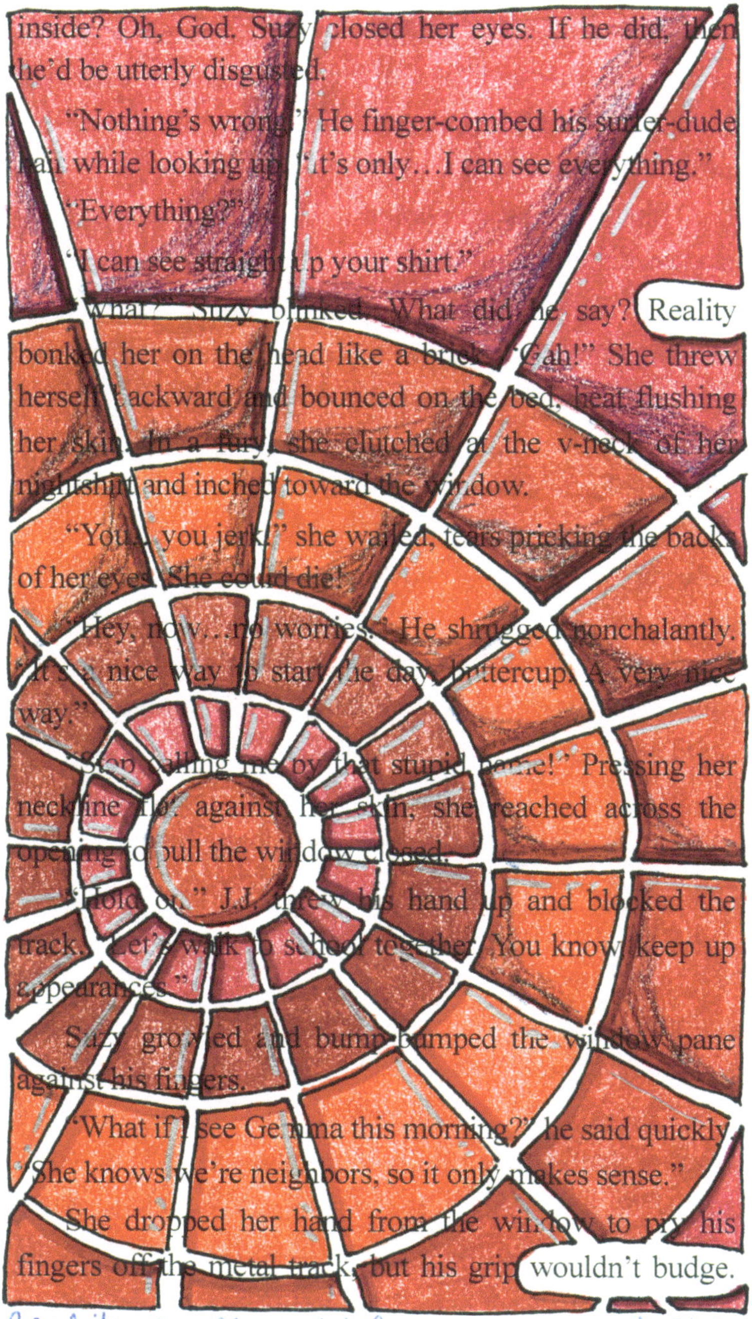

inside? Oh, God. Suzy closed her eyes. If he did, then he'd be utterly disgusted.

"Nothing's wrong." He finger-combed his surfer-dude hair while looking up. "It's only…I can see everything."

"Everything?"

"I can see straight up your shirt."

"What?" Suzy blinked. What did he say? Reality bonked her on the head like a brick. "Gah!" She threw herself backward and bounced on the bed, heat flushing her skin. In a fury, she clutched at the v-neck of her nightshirt and inched toward the window.

"You…you jerk!" she wailed, tears pricking the backs of her eyes. She could die!

"Hey, now…no worries." He shrugged nonchalantly. "It's a nice way to start the day, buttercup. A very nice way."

"Stop calling me by that stupid name!" Pressing her neckline flat against her skin, she reached across the opening to pull the window closed.

"Hold on." J.J. threw his hand up and blocked the track. "Let's walk to school together. You know, keep up appearances."

Suzy growled and bump-bumped the window pane against his fingers.

"What if I see Gemma this morning?" he said quickly. "She knows we're neighbors, so it only makes sense."

She dropped her hand from the window to pry his fingers off the metal track, but his grip wouldn't budge.

Reality by Shana Leigh July 21, 2017

THE CLOSED DOOR

Goodbye.

He stared at the closed door
where a second ago he had keys.

Single in the end.

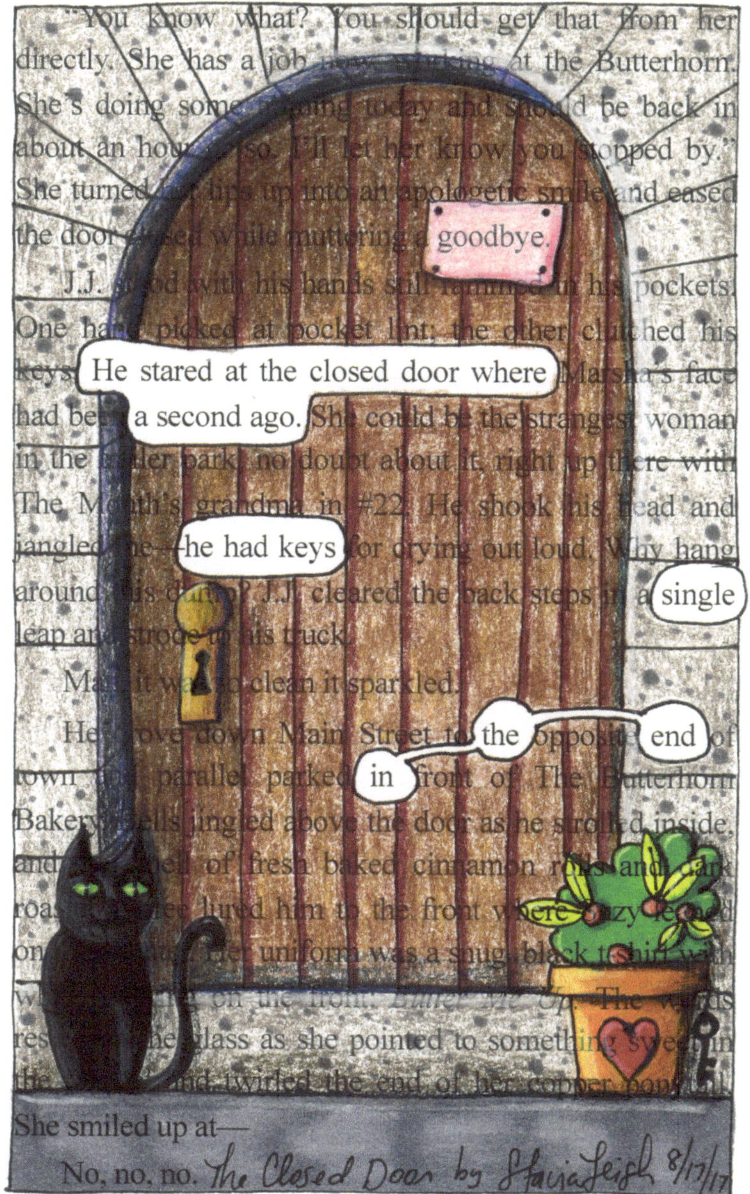
goodbye.
He stared at the closed door where
a second ago.
he had keys
single
the
end
in
The Closed Door by StaciaLeigh 8/17/17

THE LOVE CONNECTION

Love it.
Totally love tonight.
My one and only love,
drunk love, could be love, love wish,
first love.

Love sucked.
Love things, broke love…
Sounds complicated.
Love drama.
Need love? No, thanks.

Love tomorrow.
Must be love.
Night love, please…
love to have a cuddle.
Love him, in love, love you.

Lying love.
Love beer, love buddies, love her,
love feet, love guys,
love to party.
Love over. Love out.

Love time.
Kept love,
my love…
self love.

"Are you drunk?" Suzy narrowed her eyes.

"No. This is my one and only." He held up the dark bottle. "But I wish I was drunk because tonight totally ...it sucked, man. First, there was Gemma, then there wasn't. Then, I thought maybe there could be. But I said some things, you know, things I probably shouldn't have, and she broke up with me, and... no. No Gemma."

"Hmm. Sounds complicated, and as much as I'd love to stand out here in forty degree weather and chat about party drama, I need to get back in my house."

"Stay," he said, watching her. "Have a beer with me."

"No, thanks." She wrapped her arms around herself. "It's too cold."

"Alright. Tomorrow, then."

"Sure, whatever," Suzy said, shaking her head. He must be drunk. Overdale's party animal, a.k.a. Mr. Cool, was asking her to have a beer with him on a weekend night? Should she cuddle with her phone and wait for it to vibrate? Please.

"C'mon." J.J. strolled back toward the window and righted the potted plant lying on its side. "Step into my hand. I'll hike you up."

"How'd you get the beer anyway?" Suzy stepped into his clasped hands. He lifted her, and she hoisted herself in, face-planting on her bed. She pulled her feet inside and looked back out the window, down at J.J.

"Will's dad's a biker, and those guys like to party. His buddies are over all the time, so their fridge is kept

42

The Love Connection by Stacia Leigh 7/27/17

STACIA LEIGH

…grew up in the Flathead Valley and is a graduate of Montana State University. She currently resides in the Seattle area with a couple of cherrier rescue mutts, two arty farties, and a computer nerd.

Burnout is a 2016 PNWA Literary Contest finalist for young adult. Stacia's first independently published novel, *Dealing with Blue,* is a 2015 PNWA Literary Contest finalist for young adult as well as a 2016 Nancy Pearl Book Award finalist.

She enjoys writing what she loves to read, a flirty romance that's light on the angst and heavy on the fun.

Want to learn more about Stacia's upcoming books and latest projects or just want to swing by for a quick hello? Boom! Done. All you have to do is visit her here:

www.stacialeigh.com

* * *

BLACKOUT POEM

Stacia Leigh, with anticipation,
poised over the scribbles in her book.
"I've got it! A blackout poem."

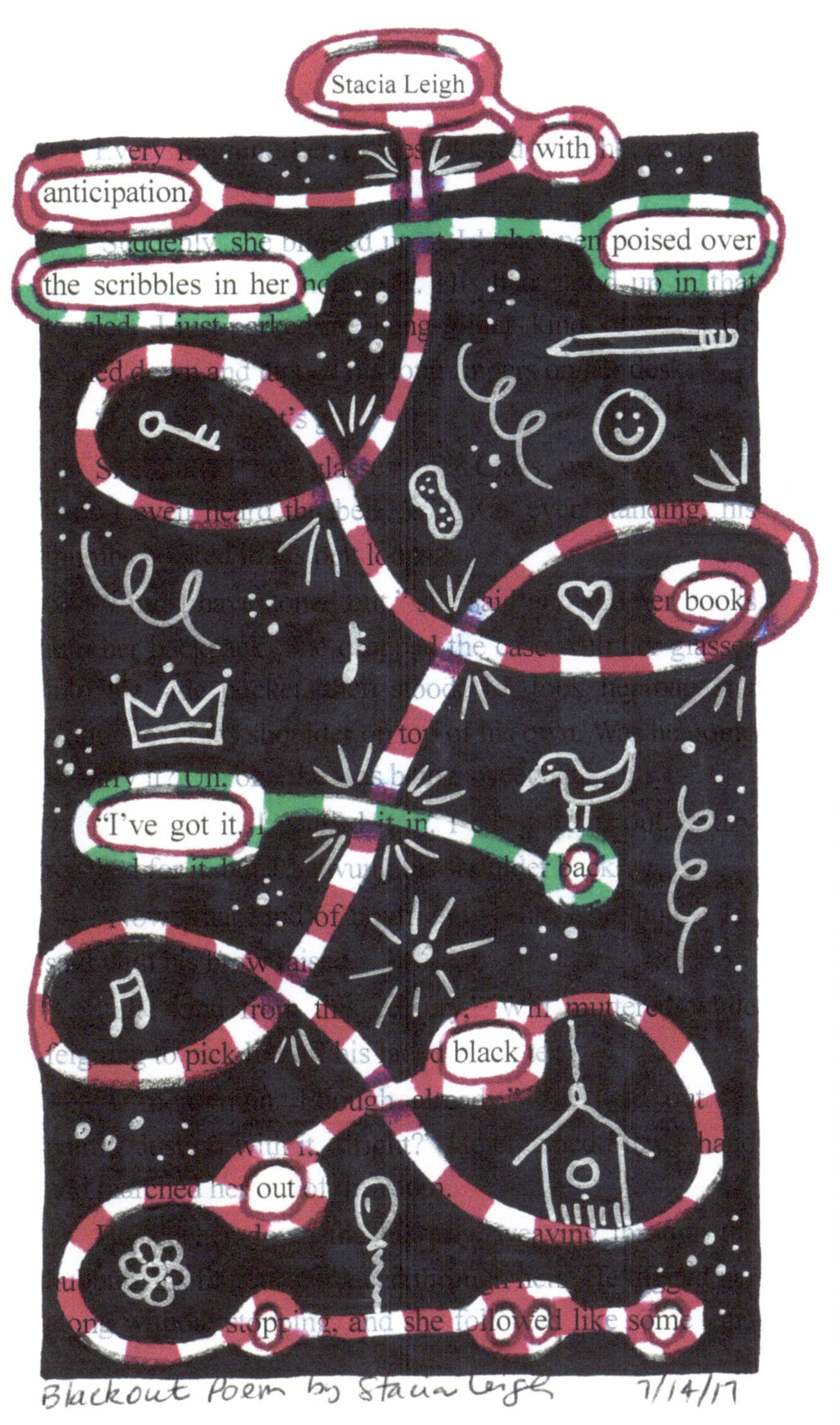
Stacia Leigh
with
anticipation.
poised over
the scribbles in her
book
"I've got it.
back
black
out
Blackout Poem by Stacia Leigh
7/14/17
164

Behind the blackout poems and doodle art are two young adult love stories with flirt, grit and small town fun. Don't miss out!

Dealing
with Blue
by
Stacia Leigh

"Name your price, Suzy Blue. Everyone's got one."— Life used to be normal until Suzy Blue moves into the trailer park with her mom. Then things turn secretive and claustrophobic. To get out of the house, Suzy accepts a deal with the charming neighbor boy, J.J. Radborne. All he needs is a pretend girlfriend for bonfires, fun, and a possible prom date, and all she needs is driving lessons to get out of this town...for good.

"You're making a huge mistake, J.J."— So says Gemma, J.J.'s ex-girlfriend. She's turning up the heat in a confusing mind game, and J.J. knows exactly who to team up with: Suzy Blue. She's cute, convenient, and even sorta funny. More importantly, Gemma's already jealous. Hey, she started it; he's just playing along. So, yeah. Suzy…perfect. Now, if she'd only cooperate.

Dealing with Blue is a small town love story set in the Pacific Northwest. It's about a strong girl and a bad boy peeling back the layers to discover what's true.

FINALIST 2015 PNWA Literary Contest for Young Adults
FINALIST 2016 PNWA Nancy Pearl Book Award

ISBN: 978-0692608814

Burnout

by
Stacia Leigh

"I have a plan."— Miki Holtz isn't some rebellious sixteen-year-old just because she dyed her hair blue and rides a motorcycle. She's an independent girl who knows what, when, and how to get things done… almost. She can't seem to gain her dad's attention or make a connection with her soul crush, Will Sullivan. But when her dad invites her along to the Burnout Biker Rally—and Will is going, too—she jumps at the chance to turn her luck around.

"I don't like the way you like me."— While grieving the death of his mom, Will Sullivan has turned into an undeniable couch potato until he's forced on a road trip with his dad's motorcycle buddies as some kind of biker therapy. What's worse? He's paired up with the prez's daughter, Miki, a girl who once humiliated him in front of his friends—a girl he can't forgive…or forget.

Burnout is an adventure story set in the Pacific Northwest where a strong girl and a moody boy discover love while trying to survive on a road trip from hell.

FINALIST for Young Adult in the 2016 PNWA Literary Contest under the title *Riding with the Hides of Hell.*

ISBN: 978-1732143500

www.ingramcontent.com/pod-product-compliance
Lightning Source LLC
LaVergne TN
LVHW052258100826
845147LV00001B/81

* 9 7 8 1 7 3 2 1 4 3 5 1 7 *